LINES DANCING

by

Mary Jones

Beleura Hill

First published 2012

Beleura Hill Books
PO Box 435
Mornington
VIC
3931
Australia

ISBN 978-0-9873074-0-8

Book design by Philip Jones
Cover illustration by the author

"In simple unadorned language, these poems reflect their author's interests and experience of life, offering considerable delight and much to contemplate."

- Joan Ackland

"'Passion,' Mary Jones writes, 'is not confined to youth' – and, then, in poems of rhythm and rhyme shows exactly what she means. The poetry of Mary Jones is full of life. It speaks of geriatric loves, loves not taken, and family. 'I am becoming my mother and my grandmother,' she notes, 'which is no bad thing.' Her best work, though, has a delightful balance of wry humour and a lightly-worn wisdom – such as her wonderful folk poems that tell fables of Pontius Pilate, the King Jasper, King Oswald the Obnoxious, and Wayne the apprentice angel – and lines that not only dance, but sing:

> *...*
> *its sides all carved with patterns rich and rare,*
> *with birds and beasts and flowers everywhere.*
> *His fingers pressed upon a secret spring*
> *and all at once the box began to sing."*

- Joel Deane

ACKNOWLEDGMENTS

'Thingy' and *'Helpline'* were performed in Poetry Idol 2009 and published in The Paradise Anthology.

'Extinction' and *'Recycling'* were both prize-winners in the South Eastern Centre for Sustainability "Go Green Slam' competition, and have been read on 3RPP Regional Radio.

'Cold Feet' was published in the anthology A Feast of Poetry 2011.

'Homecoming' was the winner of the Spotlight South West TV Brunel competition in the UK in 1970. It was read by the author on TV in the programme to commemorate the ship's return to England, and published in the magazine of The Brunel Society.

For Philip

My inspiration, editor, supporter, computer wizard and kindred spirit

LINES DANCING

The words on the page dance to and fro,
they pirouette and dosi-do,
swirl together and spring apart
and bow and curtsey with hand on heart.

Lines form and fracture and form again
of weaving women and marching men.
Patterns are clear, or lost in the mist
so nobody sees when the hand is kissed;
the shapes set fast behind iron bars
or explode and dissolve in a shower of stars.

You can square the circle and strip the willow
and put three wishes under the pillow;
just honour your partner, join the ring
and follow the lines as they dance and sing.

SOUND BOX

I keep my treasures in a box made of music.
It sings to me when I least expect it.
It has no base, no sides, no top, no corners,
but curves in on itself, enclosing not space but sound.
It opens outwards like a flower
and snaps shut into silence.

I put voices in it, but I cannot keep them long,
they escape when I am not listening.

I store my box in a vault
in a Cathedral
in a dusty cupboard under the stairs of my soul.

IN PLACES WHERE THEY SING

A terza rima to celebrate 50 years of Tudor Choristers

A seed was planted in a whispery glade
within a forest shimmering with song;
a seedling sprang and sprouted through the shade.

It grew and prospered, standing straight and strong,
tended by master-singers in their prime
who sang to it in chorus loud and long.

The sapling answered in its own sweet time
and blossomed forth in answer to their prayer
with melody and counterpoint and rhyme.

Tended with loyal and unstinting care,
over the years its roots spread wide and deep
and branches bow with fruitings rich and rare.

So now the leaves can sing the birds to sleep,
or wake the forest with a joyful cry
to make all listening creatures dance and leap.

Woodsmen will come and go as years roll by;
the tree will feed upon the skills they bring
and flourish forth new buds to multiply.

Gathering strength with each successive Spring,
its voice will soar in places where they sing.

GRUMPY OLD POET

I was brought up to parse and rhyme
and count the metre all the time;
write lines that scan, find words to fit
and follow rules of English Lit;
use proper grammar, tell it straight,
and always, always punctuate.

The poetry I now peruse,
nestling amid the weekend news,
or in slim volumes on the shelf
with foreword by the bard himself,
is praised wherever it is seen –
but what the devil does it mean?

THINGY

I'm trying to write this ... thingummy... Oh, what's the wretched word?
It's hovering, there, just out of reach... this really is absurd.
I'll get it in a minute; I know it... No, it's gone.
I'll have to change the subject – something else to focus on,
and then the word may pop back up just when I least expect it,
though it will never surface if I try to resurrect it.

Some people's minds are filing systems, organised and neat,
mine's more a sort of junk-room, overflowing round my feet,
and now as I get older, extra space is what I lack;
with each new thought I shove in, something falls out at the back.

It's words I keep forgetting, and it's mostly names of things;
without them I just flounder like a bird with broken wings.
I remember lots of fancy words, like 'zygote', 'sophomore',
and 'onomatopoeia' – but I can't remember 'door'.
So I say 'please shut the thingy,' and I use my hands a lot,
and I hope that other people know the word I just forgot.

I swear it's getting worse, I sometimes lose two words at once;
'Put the thingy on the whatsit' makes me feel a proper dunce,
and then I get so flustered I can hardly speak at all –
if I ever forget 'thingy'...well, the writing's on the wall.

This really is a problem - if I can't find words that fit,
I'll never be a poet.... Ah!... POEM, that was it!
Excuse me, I must leave now, when the muse calls I can't fight it,
'cos now I've got the bloody word, I'd better go and write it!

CHAOS THEORY

Flutter of butterfly wings
gossamer-veined
translucent
beautiful,
stirring the air with the merest whisper
less than the breath of angels,
flitting
transmitting
complex vibrations
to begin or end
a chain reaction.

Man in his ignorant wisdom
trying to change the world
sits in the playground
pulling the wings off butterflies.

EXTINCTION

Modern man fought
to the last man standing
but nature won in the end;
her weapons more powerful,
her supply of ammunition
inexhaustible.
It helped that by the finish
the men were mostly fighting one another.

The world was left to ancient man
who watched in wonder
from a safe distance,
then emerged to reclaim
his inheritance.

Now that the dust has settled,
a small dark figure
silently appears
on a rocky outcrop
in a dry red land.
He moves a bush
from the mouth of a cave
and bends to whisper to the thylacine
"You can come out now,
they've gone."

INTELLIGENT DESIGN

The iris bud softly glistened
in the early-morning dew,
delicate petals waiting to unfurl
to elegant perfection,
and the designer, proud of his creation,
went back to his drawing board
and came up with the slug.

By the same token,
why would a God with any sense at all
construct an exquisite and fragile planet
and then put man on it?

RECYCLING

Towers of newspapers topple,
 their pages blow in the breeze;
  the headlines shriek the unspeakable:
   WAR FAMINE PESTILENCE
   STUPIDITY and GREED.
  (DEATH will be along later,
he's just looking for somewhere
  to park the horse.)
   Inside pages bulge
    with triviality and tat;
   the glam, the sham, the ham.
Methodically, wearing garden gloves,
we shred and   spread and mix and turn,
'terrorism' is   reduced to 'error',
images smudge   and fall apart,
politicians drown   in coffee grounds
 and Lady Gaga   wears banana skins.
   Tearing and   shredding and
    spreading   and mixing,
    I fight a   rearguard action
   to save   the   planet,
   teaching   my   grandchildren
to make
good
com
 po
  s
  t

9

CONSEQUENCES

Eve
met Adam
in the Garden of Eden.
She said to him,
"I shall need chocolate and Botox and lots and lots of shoes."
He said to her,
"I shall need football and fast cars and weapons of mass destruction."
The consequence was
the garden was too small for them, so they left.
And the world said,
"I think I feel a headache coming on."

RECIPES

Digging out and using their old recipe books,
I am becoming my mother and my grandmother,
which is no bad thing.
Living through wars, they both made do
with what they had.
Thrift was a virtue to be valued,
and children learned to modify "I want".

Progress does not always have to be forward.
Sometimes we need a sign that says

WRONG WAY
GO BACK.

COLD FEET

She knew his dreams were dangerous and deep,
she dared not guess what currents flowed beneath.
Flinching, she thought of tentacles and teeth
and hidden caves where slimy creatures sleep.
"Trust me," he said, "I swear I won't let go.
Strike out together. We can swoop and glide
and ride the switchback of the strongest tide."
But she already felt the undertow
and so she fled, and struggled back to shore,
to venture through the depths with him no more
but stand on shifting sand and let him go.

So now she comes to soothe her weary feet,
she paddles in the shallows safe and warm,
builds castles for the lapping waves to eat
and runs for shelter at the slightest storm.

She scans the far horizon, but in vain,
the choice was made, he will not come again.
What oceans and what landfalls she has missed
pulling away from lips she should have kissed.

REKINDLING

A sonnet for PHDJ

Long had I wandered in a twilight land,
lapped in indifference, stumbling through the rain
of fading dreams, and haunted by the vain
remembrance of a hope to understand;
yet, at the touch of a companion's hand,
the soul may still be stirred to feel again
the sudden ecstasy of beauty's pain,
and all the sorrows of the drifting sand.
Such touch anew of long-forgotten fires
awakes within the soul a single spark
which, though it cannot yet match our desires,
leaves upon every part of us its mark,
and bears the hope of that from which it came –
an infinite and all-consuming flame.

THE FOUR KINGS

Caspar, and Balthazar, and Melchior;
they found a star where none had been before.
Caspar, and Melchior, and Balthazar;
to seek a king they travelled long and far.
Balthazar, Melchior, and Caspar,
and with them came a fourth, whose name was Jasper.

They rode their separate ways through bitter weather
until converging paths brought them together:
a haughty camel with a mighty king
his heavy crown all gold and glimmering;
a jet-black horse, bearing a Sultan's son
who snapped his fingers and his will was done;
an Arab stallion with a dark-browed prince,
his smile disdainful and his eyes like flints.
Caspar, and Balthazar and Melchior;
splendour like theirs was never seen before.
Melchior, Balthazar, and Caspar,
and forth to meet them, on a mule, rode Jasper.

He wore no kingly robes, no cloth of gold;
a simple cloak protected him from cold.
No train of servants followed him in dread,
no gem-encrusted crown adorned his head,
his only ornament a silver ring –
and yet his bearing showed he was a king.
They greeted him at once as one of them
and rode together, on to Bethlehem;
Balthazar, Melchior, and Caspar,
and at their side, the king whose name was Jasper.

They rode through weather treacherous and wild;
they found an inn, a stable, and a child,
and there the sumptuous princes knelt on straw
and Mary marvelled at the gifts they bore;
the jewelled caskets and the crystal flask
inviting questions that she dared not ask.
The baby slept, and did not wake or stir
as they gave gold, and frankincense, and myrrh,
heaping their richest gifts at Mary's feet

and bowing low a new-born king to greet;
Melchior, Balthazar, and Caspar,
and then, the last to bring his gift, came Jasper.

"I bring no gift of gold, like Melchior;
I rule a peasant kingdom, small and poor.
We cannot match the myrrh of Balthazar,
such costly ointment in its priceless jar,
nor can we bring you frankincense, like Caspar,
but what we have, we freely give," said Jasper,
"So now, my long and arduous journey done,
I bring a carpenter's gift, for Joseph's son."

He flung aside his cloak and doffed his hood,
knelt, and held out a little box of wood,
its sides all carved with patterns rich and rare,
with birds and beasts and flowers everywhere.
His fingers pressed upon a secret spring
and all at once the box began to sing.
It opened to reveal a fragile bird,
whose carved wings fluttered as its song was heard.
He held the singing bird above the child,
who woke, and heard its silvery notes, and smiled.
The kings all marvelled at the maker's art,
and Jasper spoke, direct to Mary's heart.

"Rich are the gifts these other kings have brought,
and you must hold their message in your thought.
He shall be king, and God, and born to die,
just as their precious presents prophesy,
but see the gift I bring, and mark it too:
he shall be human, and bring joy to you
with simple craft, with laughter and with love,
delighting earth below and heaven above."

The kings departed and went on their way,
but Mary often thought about that day;
the humble stable filled with wondrous things,
the night air ringing with the speech of kings;
Balthazar, Melchior, and Caspar –
but most of all, Mary remembered Jasper.

PILATE

after Carol Ann Duffy's 'Pilate's Wife'

The deal was done already; all worked out,
to soothe the temple priests and protect Rome.
The mob would be placated, either way,
and Caiaphas's men were standing by.

The Nazarene was doomed. Barabbas too.
Whichever was released would 'disappear'.
An insurrection quietly defused;
Caesar and Herod doubly satisfied.

It should have been no problem. Every day
I make decisions and my word is law.
I am a diplomat; I'm good at this,
the politics, the compromise, the spin.

But then – my wife. What does she know of law?
How can she dare to interfere like this?
I chose her for her skin, her eyes, her hair.
I never thought to meet a mind and will.

Why did I listen? She should keep her dreams
and portents to herself, they don't scare me.
I was a fool to heed her; twice a fool
to be persuaded I should see the man.

Well, I have seen him; looked into his eyes.
That face will haunt me till the day I die.
It makes no difference now, his fate is sealed,
but how I dread his blood upon my hands.

I always knew this job would make my name,
but now I see my future veiled in shame.

DUET

We are not often noted
for our harmony,
but boy, do we do counterpoint.

COMMITMENT IN THE 21ST CENTURY

Now and then
here and there
by and large
give or take
one way or another
all things considered
I think
I probably
love
you

take it
or leave it.

VICIOUS CIRCLE

A villanelle for a lost relationship

I do not love you any more.
You squeezed my heart and made it crack.
That's what I can't forgive you for.

When you walked out, you slammed the door.
You said you're never coming back.
I do not love you any more.

You were my angel to adore.
Now you've stretched me on the rack.
That's what I can't forgive you for.

Nothing is how it was before.
We've both said words we can't take back.
I do not love you any more.

Your darts have pierced me to the core.
You caught me in a stealth attack.
That's what I can't forgive you for.

I stand upon a rocky shore.
My mood is blue, my thoughts are black.
I do not love you any more –
that's what I can't forgive you for.

CLUTTER

Rubbish accumulates.

We have cupboards full of old grudges,
drawers stuffed with resentment,
shelves piled high with prejudice,
boxes overflowing
with disappointment and regret.

"If only", we say, "we had more space
to keep all this in order,
then how much happier we would be."

Actually
we don't need storage space at all.
We just need to learn
to throw our junk away.

THE PASSIONATE GERIATRIC TO HIS LOVE

with apologies to Christopher Marlowe, whose first line it is, and to John Donne, Cecil Day Lewis and Ogden Nash, who all pinched it before I did.

Come live with me and be my love
and I will thank the Gods above
for sending you to cuddle me
and sit on my arthritic knee.

I'll lay my pension at your feet,
buy violets every time we meet,
and take you travelling everywhere
with Seniors discounts on our fare.

Move into my retirement flat
and on my hat-stand hang your hat;
just leave your Zimmer in my hall,
and I will catch you if you fall.

We'll tango, sensuous and slow,
to music from the radio.
Forget about your dodgy hips
and pucker up your ancient lips.

I'll turn my batteries up to hear
you mumble softly in my ear,
and then my cardigan I'll doff
and help you take your corsets off.

Come park your slippers on my rug,
I'll bring you Horlicks in a mug,
and you can rest your snow-white head
upon my orthopaedic bed.

Passion is not confined to youth;
on bedside table see the truth
to show the world what's come to pass -
two sets of dentures in one glass!

HE SAID, SHE SAID

The Way Home

"My memory's perfectly fine," he said,
"I know just where we are.
So I'll get us home in no time at all –
when I find where I've parked the car."

Height/Weight Tables

"I'm not really overweight," she said,
"it isn't a problem at all.
It's just that I ought to be a man
who's six-foot-seven tall."

End-game

"I'm not a grand master at chess," he said,
"I know losing isn't a sin,
but what really rankles is the fact
that my son has just let me win."

Mother Love

"My daughter needs all my care," she said.
"She couldn't survive without me,"
(ignoring the fact that she's ninety six
and her daughter's seventy three.)

Bombshell

"I have a confession to make," he said,
"I hope it won't ruin your life.
I've plucked up the courage to leave you at last,
and I'm going back home to my wife."

Footnote

"I try to keep up with fashion," she said,
"but it causes me endless woes.
There's no room, in a shoe by Jimmy Choo,
for a bunion and hammer toes."

KING OSWALD

King Oswald-the-Obnoxious was a really nasty king.
He was beastly to his subjects; made them squeal like anything.
He clobbered them with taxes, and he made them dig his garden;
he was rude to everybody and he never begged their pardon;
he wouldn't let them dance or sing or anything like that,
and he often lost his temper, and kicked the Palace cat.
He was greedy, mean and spiteful, and on top of all these vices,
each summer when the sun came out he banned the sale of ices.
The people in his kingdom didn't have a lot of fun;
he made them work hard all the time, and when the work was done
he let them have one holiday in every seven years,
but only if they brought him back exotic souvenirs.

One day, there came to Oswald's court a prince from far off lands.
He had a helmet on his head, and gauntlets on his hands,
but he didn't have a horse, a suit of armour, sword or pike.
No, he wore a leather jacket and he rode a motor bike.
He screeched up to the Palace gates, and when they let him in
he marched right up to Oswald and he asked him, with a grin,
"Do you have by any chance a fearsome dragon I can slaughter,
in return for half your kingdom and a wedding with your daughter?"
Now, Oswald had no daughter, 'cos he didn't have a wife.
(No woman in her right mind would put up with all that strife.)
He told the prince, who said, "Oh well, in that case, I'll be off."
"Oh no you won't!" said Oswald, with a pompous little cough.
"You don't get out of here, my lad, without a guarantee
that you'll go on a quest to find some treasure just for me,
and if you don't, you'll find yourself in jail in seconds flat."
The prince got quite indignant, and he said, "You can't do that!"
"Look, I'm the king round here," said Oswald, "I do what I like,
and just to make sure you come back, I'll confiscate your bike.
Be back here by next Thursday, prompt at twenty five past four,
and bring me something priceless that I've never had before."
The prince just raised one eyebrow, and gave a languid sigh,
and then approached the king and looked him squarely in the eye.
"O.K.," he said, "I'll do just that; it's not too hard a task.
In fact, I think you'll find I do exactly what you ask."
He strode away, and rode away upon a borrowed horse,
leaving his precious bike - a Harley Davidson, of course.

Next Thursday, at the appointed time, the prince came riding back,
and slung across his saddle he had something in a sack.
He burst into the Palace and he strode up to the king,
and placed the sack before him and untied the knotted string.
Then from the sack emerged the most amazing little creature,
which didn't seem to have one single ordinary feature.
Its feet were black, its hands were blue, its face was pink and puffy,
its body green with purple spots, its front all soft and fluffy,
but on its back were prickly spikes, of orange tipped with red,
which matched the orange feathers in the plume upon its head.
The courtiers gasped; the king cried, "Blimey, what on earth is that?
I said bring me some treasure, you pathetic little brat!"
"And so I have," the prince replied. "Just as you told me to.
This precious thing's your conscience, reared especially for you.
It's priceless, it's exclusive, and you've not had one before;
it's exactly what you needed, so who could ask for more?
Just let me introduce you; he's a lovely little chappie,
and if you treat him right I'm sure you'll both be very happy."
The conscience wagged its back end, chirped, and jumped on Oswald's
    knee.
It dug its claws into his robes and climbed him like a tree.
It perched upon his shoulder and it nibbled at his ear,
and Oswald's face went purple as he roared in rage and fear,
"You'll pay for this, you wretched boy. Guards! Throw the prince in
    jail!"
Then the conscience raised its prickles and let out a mighty wail.
It roared and screeched and hollered and it made a frightful din,
and it wouldn't stop until the king said, "All right, I give in.
Just give him back his bike and get him right away from here,
I never want to see him here again, is that quite clear?"
The prince said, "Just calm down a bit; that conscience is your friend,
and when you get to know him you will thank me in the end.
I'm really very sorry if his noise gives you a fright,
but the only way to shut him up is just to do what's right."
He leapt upon his bike, then grinned and shouted, "Ta ta mates!"
did a wheely in the courtyard, and skidded through the gates.
He roared off to another kingdom, seeking fame and glory.
(He rescued Sleeping Beauty there - but that's another story.)

From that day on, King Oswald was a very different man,
and soon throughout the kingdom a new happy age began,
for every time the king slipped back into his nasty ways,
his conscience screeched and yelled at him, and pestered him for days.
So gradually he mellowed, and he led a better life,
until he got so lovable, he even found a wife.
He took care of his conscience; it became a much loved pet,
and he changed his name by deed poll, all his past crimes to forget.
And so his kingdom grew in health and wealth and song and laughter,
and King Maurice-the-Magnanimous ruled happy ever after.

LIMBO DANCING

I am subtle
I am supple
I can sneak beneath the bar.

Under the bar and over the edge
worming my way back from the recycle bin
every time.

Don't talk to me of original sin
I invented it.
I was there when the apple was tasted, remember,
but I swore afterwards that it wasn't my fault.

And now,
when all the angels are busy dancing
through the eye of a needle,
on my belly I shall go.
I shall lead the holy innocents
under the bar and over the edge
and out of limbo
while nobody is looking.

COMPANY SONG

(To be sung to the tune 'Battle-hymn of the Republic', with chorus 'Glory, Glory Hallelujah!')

From the humblest little tea-boy to the Chairman of the Board,
let us gather here together; let us sing with one accord
the praises of the Company by all of us adored.
Our firm is marching on.

The business has been flourishing since 1894
making little metal nuts that have a thirteen-sided bore,
and nobody remembers now exactly what they're for
but we still go marching on.

The time-and-motion experts find our methods out of date,
and accountants say our books are in a pretty hopeless state.
It would take about a century to put our records straight
but we keep on marching on.

Though modern business methods give our confidence a jolt,
the thought will still sustain us, when we're tempted to revolt,
that somewhere there's a firm that makes a thirteen-sided bolt
so we just keep marching on.

HELPLINE

If you're lost and on the run,
please press button number 1.

If you don't know what to do,
please press button number 2.

If you're searching for the key,
please press button number 3.

If you can't cope any more,
please press button number 4.

But if you crave a human voice
for sympathy or friendly chat,
we're afraid you have no choice –
our buttons do not cover that.

We're sorry if our options cause you pain.
Press hash, and you can hear them all again.

Your call *is* important to us... click.
Your call *is* important to us... click.
Your call *is* important to us... click.

Beeeeeeeeeeeeeep.

HOMECOMING

A celebration of the return to England in 1970 of Brunel's ship 'The Great Britain'

Battered and bruised and barnacle-bedecked,
she reaches home to cheers and welcoming flags;
a beauty queen returned in tattered rags
but still a queen, and worthy of respect.
Once she was fêted, wondered at, adored.
Now, weary with the chains of time, she stands
patient beneath the touch of healing hands
to have her youthful finery restored.
Rejuvenation beckons her, and yet
no restoration could improve upon
the pride and majesty that now she wears;
the timeless beauty none will dare forget
of line and structure perfectly at one
burns through the ravaged face and all its cares.

DEATHCAP

Children are gambolling over green fields
gathering mushrooms.

Visions of innocence scatter and fade
dissolving in close-up.
Echoes of laughter are lost in the shade
of greed and corruption,
never returning.

Children are bickering under blue skies,
gathering storm-clouds.

Spores of destruction drift on the breeze
respecting no boundaries.
Death-seeking filaments finger the trees,
thread through the undergrowth, sink into sub-soil,
questing and yearning.

Young men are threatening under grey skies,
gathering darkness.

Deep in dank cellars the buttons sprout,
tended by old men
hunkered in bunkers, suppressing all doubt,
gambling the future,
never learning.

Mushrooms are gambolling over black fields
gathering children.

SQUATTERS

A family of gremlins has moved in with me
and sometimes I feel I shall never be free.
They hide things; they break things; they lose things; and so
I want them to leave, but I can't make them go.

They love to hide papers, or shuffle the pages,
so the one that I search for goes missing for ages,
and then, when my temper is thoroughly cooked,
they put it back, right in the place I first looked.

They nest in dark corners and make themselves dens.
There's one in my handbag, he eats ball-point pens.
The one in the laundry is sly like a fox,
he spends his life munching up piles of odd socks.

The one in the dish-washer's really quite mean,
he puts dirty crockery in with the clean.
There are two in the garden, when they're on the prowl
I get all confused; they keep moving my trowel.

There's one sneaky creature who lives in the car
and makes sure I never know where my keys are;
He passes them back to the living room, where
his mates stash them right down the side of a chair.

They're driving me mad with their pranks and their tricks
but I think I can see a way out of this fix.
I'll trap them in poems, expose them to view,
and hope they'll transfer their attentions to you.

LADIES WHO LUNCH

The restaurant at the winery
is filled with chatter,
the Muzak of low voices
a gentle background hum.
The descant startles when it first erupts
in shrieks of laughter.
Heads are turned towards the window table
where the flock has settled.
The noise continues
while they peck at salads,
sipping wine,
easing off, under the table,
elegantly uncomfortable shoes.
Their voices soar and swoop,
shrilling and spilling,
filling the air around them.
They share dessert,
retrieve capacious handbags from the floor,
split the bill
and are gone in a flurry of air kisses.

Colourful and gregarious;
several species may feed together.
Voice: noisy screech while in flight,
more pleasant note while feeding.
Locally abundant.
Common in parkland and in gardens -
and in wineries.

CONKERS

The board-room table is mahogany,
dark, smooth, cool beneath my fingers.
I caress it and the texture speaks to me
of conkers, that no child of mine
will ever now delight in.

I have presented my report,
powerful men await my conclusions
but for this moment I am dumb.

I have run seminars on management techniques;
I thought that I could manage my own life.
Glass ceilings were no obstacle to me,
I shattered them.
They sent their icy slivers through my heart
but I was unperturbed.
Gaining a partnership I lost a partner
but I was still invulnerable.

The clinic was expensive and discreet.
The doctor had a table just like this
but smaller.
I did not think of conkers then
as I made the executive decision.

I sweep my notes together and continue.
They have not seen me hesitate
and so my reputation is intact.

From here there is no other way but this,
crossing the danger zones in frozen calm
to reach the dizzy heights of my career,
each of my moments now a little death.

POST-OP PANTOUM

It's one step forward, two steps back.
The pain is mainly in my head,
I'll laugh at this along the track –
or so my physiotherapist said.

The pain is mainly in my head,
relax and set my muscles free,
or so my physiotherapist said.
That's fine for him – it's not his knee.

Relax and set my muscles free,
release the tissue, stretch the scar.
That's fine for him, it's not his knee
that screams when I get in the car.

Release the tissues, stretch the scar,
just keep on working through the pain
that screams when I get in the car,
then rest, and do it all again.

Just keep on working through the pain,
I'll laugh at this along the track,
then rest and do it all again;
it's two steps forward, one step back.

TRAVELLING HOPEFULLY

The train now standing at Platform Four
is likely to stand there for evermore.
A replacement service may be found
at one of the platforms underground,
but I shan't tell you which one it's on
until just after the train has gone.

The train expected at Platform Eight
is running an hour and a quarter late.
There's no other service from this station
to that particular destination.
It's no good swearing and making a fuss,
you'd better go off and look for a bus.

The train now arriving at Platform Ten
will stop for a while and pull out again.
It's route's been changed to I don't know where
but it's not what the timetable says, so there!
If you find yourself travelling on the wrong track
you must get off and wait for the next train back.

There won't be a train on Platform Three
because it's now been cancelled, you see.
I suppose you'd like to be told what's next
but you'll just have to watch the scrolling text.
My shift has ended, so that is that -
I'm getting a taxi back home to my flat.

BORDER CONTROL

The problem is deciding
what is weed and what is not.
In a herbaceous border run to seed
the thugs and hoons are obvious;
easy to recognise, hard to control,
insidious, stubborn, spreading underground.
You zap them here,
they spring up somewhere else.
Imported or native, makes no difference,
they need vigilance and constant warfare.

If you want to be strict about it,
and many people do,
the treasured rose-bush
from an old colonial garden,
the Mediterranean lavender
thriving in the southern sun,
camellias from China and Japan,
exotics from deep jungles far away,
could all be classed as weeds,
but they make their contributions,
working their way
into the national landscape.

It all depends
on what you mean
by 'invasive'.

MATESHIP

Whitefella wandering out in the bright sun,
stumbling through spinifex,
drifting in circles.
Silly bugger be dead soon.
Can't just let him go under.
Better show him where the water is.

Whitefella blundering up in the blue hills,
looking for trackways,
hacking and staggering.
Silly bugger be lost soon.
Can't just let him go under.
Better show him the way through.

Whitefella rooting around in the red dirt,
planting his strange crops
in the wrong season.
Silly bugger'll starve soon.
Can't just let him go under.
Better show him how to find tucker.

Blackfella sniffing gas out on the dark street,
reeking of alcohol,
coughing and mumbling.
Silly bugger be dead soon.
Better just let him go under.
That'll show him.

BULLIES

They seem to set each other off,
gang up on me and do their worst together.
When one's away, the other's not so bad,
and there are days,
oh, blessed days,
when neither of the cruel pair
is there.

Mostly, though, each morning
they both announce their presence,
so I know
the day will be a battle
and an unsuccessful flight,
until they saunter home with me
and slide into my bed at night,
nudging and pinching at my side
long after I turn out the light.

My left hip and my right knee
have allied and declared a war on me,
a war of sieges and attrition.
I can still defeat them
by the power of my will.
If I just ignore them
they fade into the background,
and I can pretend they are not there.
This is my secret weapon.
A sort of hip-knee-sis.

PIN NUMBER

The bank says I have to be careful,
look after my card and my PIN,
I must guard the entry to my account
so nobody else can get in.

I mustn't keep cards together
or write down the numbers at all
so I stand here all of a dither
in front of the slot in the wall.

It shouldn't be hard to remember
four numbers, for heaven's sake,
but they have to be in the right order
so it's easy to make a mistake.

I didn't just pick them at random;
it's 8 for the age of my cat,
(of course, he'll be 9 next September
So what shall I do about that?)

Then there's 3 for my lovely grand-children
and 4 for the date we were wed
and 7 for no good reason at all
but it just popped into my head.

So 8743 was my first try,
after thinking ever so hard,
then 8734, and 4738 -
and now it won't give back my card.

So I'll have to go in there and ask them,
and I don't understand why on earth
they need to have sight of my passport
and ask me the date of my birth.

They've explained about theft of identity,
but I really can't quite see
why anyone in the criminal world
could possibly want to be me.

I suppose the banks know what they're doing,
but I can't get it straight in my head,
so I think I'll just do what my dear mother did –
keep it under the mattress instead.

WAYNE

If you ever think of Angels, that bright band of heavenly brothers,
you may not know, some angels are more heavenly than others.
There's a certain pecking order in the Lord's celestial choir,
for though all angels sit on high, a few sit even higher.
Archangels get the highest billing in the heavenly show,
and after them the Seraphim, in order high to low;
below them are the common Angels; under them again
come the smallest of the Cherubim; and under them .... there's Wayne.
Now Wayne is an apprentice on an Angel Training Scheme.
He's spotty, small, and none too bright, but still he has a dream:
he wants to bring to humankind the news of peace and joy.
He's in Gabriel's department, as a junior errand boy.

One Christmas, Gabriel said to Wayne, "It's time you had a try
at bearing tidings by yourself, so come on, don't be shy.
I know you're not too confident, but why not have a shot?
Just go for it, my lad, and give it everything you've got."
"I will," said Wayne, and flew to earth, determined to do well,
and overjoyed to have the chance God's messages to tell.

Alas for Wayne! The world has changed a lot since Gabriel's day.
No simple shepherds in the fields Wayne found upon his way,
but crowded cities, packed with people suffering from stress
who wouldn't hear Wayne's voice - in fact they couldn't listen less.
So when he hovered in the sky and sang, "Good news I bring!"
he soon felt rather foolish; no one saw or heard a thing.
"O.K.," he thought, "my first mistake. I see I've aimed too high.
I'm really not high-powered enough to try to fill the sky.
I'll need to set my sights a little lower, I suppose;
I'll pick a smaller group of people first, see how that goes."
He focused on one household, and he really tried his best.
He sang outside their door for hours, without a stop for rest.
He shouted through the letter box; he tapped the window pane;
then paused for thought, and soared up to the roof to try again.
He tumbled down the chimney, and with soot upon his wings
he fluttered round their living room and sang of wondrous things.
But no one even noticed him, as round their heads he flew;
they were all glued to the telly, watching "Terminator 2".

A sadly disappointed Wayne next tried the Christmas shops,
but there he fared no better, though he pulled out all the stops.
The more he tried to broadcast joyful tidings far and wide,
the more the hurrying shoppers pushed him callously aside.
He was muddy and bedraggled, with his wings still stained with soot,
and he only just avoided getting trampled underfoot.
Twice people poked him in the eye with sprigs of festive holly,
and once he got bowled over by a charging Coles's trolley.
At last he found his way inside a massive Superstore,
and suddenly he knew he couldn't stand it any more.
He perched upon a high shelf where the tinsel balls were kept
and, cold and tired and miserable, he hung his head and wept.

Then, as he sat and sobbed until his wingtips gently shook,
he heard a gasp of wonder, and a voice said, "Mummy, LOOK!
An angel! It's an angel," and a child stood there before him.
Wayne's heart leapt up; his sobbing stopped - at last, somebody saw
    him.
Her mother said, "Oh no, my dear, it's very plain to me,
it's just a rather scruffy ornament to hang upon the tree."
The little girl looked up at Wayne; her wide eyes never blinked,
and then he slowly raised his head, and looked at her, and winked.
She clapped her hands with joy, and cried, "Oh Mummy, can't you see?
He's a really truly angel, and he's looking straight at me."
The mother smiled indulgently, and turned her daughter round,
but not before the child saw something floating to the ground.
The girl bent down and picked it up, and as they left together,
her fingers clutched one single, shining, slightly sooty feather.

When Wayne reported back, the Angel Gabriel said, "Well done.
We'll make an angel of you yet - you're getting there, my son."
So if one day you hear the message that the angel brings
from a rather spotty messenger with slightly grubby wings,
please listen to him carefully, then as he flies away
just give the lad a friendly wave - you'll really make his day.

BEDSPREAD

Two threads entwined and knitted up together
dancing between Fate's needles,
now in a wild fandango,
now a stately waltz.
The colours shift and swirl and variegate;
Sometimes they complement each other
sometimes they clash,
and here and there a thread is touched
with purest gold.

In places
one of the threads is weaker than the other
and there are spots where both are wearing thin,
but still the lineage remains unbroken;
the overall effect,
viewed with the benefit of time and distance,
an heirloom for the family to cherish.

Stronger together than ever they were apart,
They crafted an enduring work of art.

DEFINITION OF A POEM

A sudden vortex
in the cerebral cortex,
cutting a temporary caper
on paper.

NOTES ON THE POEMS

IN PLACES WHERE THEY SING : The Tudor Choristers was founded in Melbourne in 1962. It is a small choir specialising in unaccompanied music, and has established a reputation as one of Australia's finest choral ensembles.

CONSEQUENCES : 'Consequences' is a Victorian parlour game where each player adds one more line before folding the paper and passing it on to the next person. The elements of the story can vary but always include two people, where they met, what they said and the consequences, often ending with 'and the world said…'

THE PASSIONATE GERIATRIC TO HIS LOVE : Christopher Marlowe wrote 'The Passionate Shepherd to his Love', and Sir Walter Raleigh wrote 'The Nymph's Reply to the Shepherd'. 'The Bait' by John Donne, 'Song' by Cecil Day Lewis and 'Love under the Republicans (or Democrats)' by Ogden Nash all use the same first line, which has also inspired many other poems and song lyrics.

HOMECOMING : Brunel's ship SS Great Britain was brought back to Bristol in 1970 from the Falkland Islands, where she had been scuttled in 1937. She was towed up the river Avon, passing under Brunel's Clifton Suspension Bridge, to the dry dock where she was first built in the early 1840's. She has been restored to her former glory and is now open to the public.

WAYNE: The supermarket trolley started life as belonging to Tesco. Since arriving in Australia it has switched allegiance to Coles. It was either that or Woolworths, but that would have all the wrong connotations for UK readers.

ABOUT THE AUTHOR

Mary Jones doesn't believe in taking the direct path anywhere, usually preferring the scenic route. That's why she studied Science subjects at school, took an Arts degree, taught Maths and got involved in theatre.

Her short stories have been published, read on radio, translated, and plagiarised. She's won competitions, but the pleasure of winning doesn't come anywhere near the joy of hearing an audience laugh at a line she's written.

In the three years that she's lived in Australia, she's written more poems than she did in the previous fifty – perhaps there's something in the air.

'Lines Dancing' is her first poetry collection.

www.ingramcontent.com/pod-product-compliance
Lightning Source LLC
LaVergne TN
LVHW041209080426
835508LV00008B/871